Baritone/Bass
Volume 2

THE SINGERS MUSICAL THEATRE ANTHOLOGY

A collection of songs from the musical stage, categorized by voice type. The selections are presented in their authentic settings, excerpted from the original vocal scores.

Compiled and Edited by Richard Walters

HAL•LEONARD®
CORPORATION
7777 W. BLUEMOUND RD. P.O. BOX 13819 MILWAUKEE, WI 53213

5-2332-X

FOREWORD

As the century nears its end, it is apparent to me that the most important and lasting body of performable American music for singers has come from the musical theatre and musical film. The classical tradition as it has been continued in the United States in this century has produced few major composers who have written extensively for the voice, producing a relatively small body of sometimes profound and beautiful literature, but often relevant only to specialized audiences. In pre-rock era popular traditions, the songs that were not written for the stage or film are largely inferior in quality to those written for Broadway and Hollywood (although there are plenty of exceptions to this general rule). Perhaps the reason is simply that the top talent was attracted to and nurtured by those two venues, and inspired by the best performers. But it's also possible that writing for a character playing some sort of scene, no matter how thin the dramatic context (sometimes undetectable), has inherently produced better songs. Compare a Rodgers and Hart ballad from the 1930s (which are all from musicals) to just an average pop ballad from that time not from the stage or screen, if you can dig one up, and you might see what I mean. Popular music of the rock era, primarily performers writing dance music for themselves to record, is almost a completely different aesthetic, and is most often ungratifying for the average singer to present in a typical performance with piano accompaniment.

The five volumes that comprise the original edition of *The Singer's Musical Theatre Anthology,* released in 1987, contain many of the most famous songs for a voice type, as well as being peppered with some more unusual choices. Volume two of the series allows a deeper investigation into the available literature. I have attempted to include a wide range of music, appealing to many different tastes and musical and vocal needs. As in the first volumes, whenever possible the songs are presented in what is their most authentic setting, excerpted from the vocal score or piano/rehearsal score, in the key originally performed and with the original piano accompaniment arrangement (which is really a representation of the orchestra, of course, although Kurt Weill was practically the only Broadway composer to orchestrate his own shows). A student of this subject will notice that these accompaniments are quite a bit different from the standard sheet music arrangements that were published of many of these songs, where the melody is put into a simplified piano part and moved into a convenient and easy piano key, without much regard to vocal range.

In the first volume of the series, I tried to walk a fine line in the mezzo-soprano choices, attempting to accomodate a mix of how theatre people define that voice type —almost exclusively meaning belting — and how classical tradition defines mezzo-soprano. In volume two I have restricted the choices to songs for a belting range, although they don't necessarily need to be belted, and put any songs sung in what theatre people call "head voice" or "soprano voice" in the soprano volume. As was true in the first volume, classically trained mezzo-sopranos will be comfortable with many of the songs in the soprano book.

The "original" keys are presented here, although that often means only the most comfortable key for the original performer. Transpositions of this music are perfectly acceptable. Some songs in these volumes might be successfully sung by any voice type. Classical singers and teachers using these books should remember that the soprano tessitura of this style of material, which often seems very low, was a deliberate aesthetic choice, aimed at clarity of diction, often done to avoid a cultured sound in a singing voice inappropriate to the desired character of the song and role, keeping what I term a Broadway ingenue range. Barbara Cook and Julie Andrews are famous examples of this kind of soprano, with singing concentrated in an expressive and strong middle voice. Also regarding tessituras, some men may find comfortable songs in both the tenor and baritone volumes, in a "baritenor" range, typically with a top note of G.

It's exciting to present songs in this new edition that have never before appeared in print. Many great songs still hold the stage, even if many of the shows don't. The nine volumes of the series present 358 songs from 117 musicals, dating from 1905 to 1991. It's a small percentage of our theatre heritage, but is still a comprehensive and relatively representative sampling of the stage music of New York, and to a much lesser degree London, in the twentieth century.

Many people have been kind and helpful to me in my research and preparation of this edition. They will forgive me if I only mention my debt of gratitude to the late musical theatre historian Stanley Green. I was fortunate enough to work with him as his editor on his last two books. Stanley's grasp of the subject, his compelling prose, and his high standards of research continue to inspire me.

Richard Walters, editor
May, 1993

THE SINGER'S MUSICAL THEATRE ANTHOLOGY
Baritone/Bass
Volume 2

Contents

ANNIE GET YOUR GUN
14   The Girl That I Marry
16   My Defenses Are Down

ANYTHING GOES
20   All Through the Night

BELLS ARE RINGING
26   Long Before I Knew You
29   Just in Time

THE BOYS FROM SYRACUSE
36   This Can't Be Love

CAN-CAN
33   It's All Right With Me

CAROUSEL
40   The Highest Judge of All

DO RE MI
44   All of My Life

GENTLEMEN PREFER BLONDES
51   Bye Bye Baby

GUYS AND DOLLS
54   My Time of Day
56   Luck Be a Lady
66   More I Cannot Wish You

JESUS CHRIST SUPERSTAR
69   Pilate's Dream

KISMET
72   Fate

KISS ME, KATE
78   I've Come to Wive it Wealthily in Padua

KNICKERBOCKER HOLIDAY
84   There's Nowhere to Go But Up

LITTLE MARY SUNSHINE
90   You're the Fairest Flower

A LITTLE NIGHT MUSIC
95   In Praise of Women

MACK AND MABEL
102   I Won't Send Roses

ME AND MY GIRL
106   Leaning on a Lamp-Post

MERRILY WE ROLL ALONG
112   Good Thing Going

LES MISÉRABLES
124   Empty Chairs at Empty Tables
128   Stars

MLLE. MODISTE
148   I Want What I Want When I Want It

THE MOST HAPPY FELLA
117   Joey, Joey, Joey

MY FAIR LADY
152   I've Grown Accustomed to Her Face

NINE
133   Guido's Song
142   Only With You

OKLAHOMA!
164   The Surrey with the Fringe on Top

OLIVER!
184   My Name

ON THE TOWN
190   Lonely Town

PIPE DREAM
175   All At Once You Love Her
178   The Man I Used to Be

PROMISES, PROMISES
220   Promises, Promises

SHE LOVES ME
196   Ilona

SILK STOCKINGS
202   All of You

STREET SCENE
206   Wouldn't You Like to Be on Broadway

THE UNSINKABLE MOLLY BROWN
212   I'll Never Say No

WHERE'S CHARLEY
216   Once in Love with Amy

ABOUT THE SHOWS

ANNIE GET YOUR GUN

Music and Lyrics: Irving Berlin
Book: Herbert and Dorothy Fields
Director: Joshua Logan
Choreographer: Helen Tamiris
Opened: 5/16/46, New York; a run of 1,147 performances

Originally Jerome Kern was to have written the score with Dorothy Fields doing the lyrics. After his death, Berlin was brought in to the task, which was an unusual undertaking for him. Berlin had never written the entire score to a book musical such as "Annie." Written to highlight the talents of Broadway star Ethel Merman, the show is about Annie Oakley, a hillbilly, who joins Buffalo Bill's traveling Wild West Show. She falls for the show's star shooter, Frank Butler, but complicates their romance by rivalling him as the better shot and the bigger attraction. At a shooting contest with Frank near the end of the show, she finally realizes that the only way to get her man is to let him win. The movie version was originally to have starred Judy Garland, but after she was fired from the set, Betty Hutton played the role on screen opposite Howard Keel in the 1950 release. A new recording of the musical was released in 1990.

ANYTHING GOES

Music and Lyrics: Cole Porter
Book: Guy Bolton & P.G. Wodehouse, Howard Lindsay & Russel Crouse
Director: Howard Lindsay
Choreographer: Robert Alton
Opened: 11/21/34, New York; a run of 420 performances

Cole Porter's best score of the 1930s is a fun-filled story taking place on an ocean liner about a group of oddball characters, including a nightclub singer, an enamoured stow away, a debutante, and an underworld criminal disguised as a clergyman. Featuring a fresh, young Ethel Merman, the show was one of the biggest hits of its time, containing such hits as the title song, "You're the Top," "I Get a Kick Out of You," "Blow, Gabriel, Blow," and "All Through the Night." *Anything Goes* played Off Broadway in a 1962 production (239 performances), and enjoyed its biggest success in a 1987 Broadway revival starring Patti LuPone (804 performances). There is a 1936 filmed version, and another movie from 1956 with the title *Anything Goes,* but which bears little resemblance to the original. An excellent new recording, faithful to the 1934 original production, was released in the 1980s featuring Frederica Von Stade, Cris Groenendaal, and Kim Criswell.

BELLS ARE RINGING

Music: Jule Styne
Book and Lyrics: Betty Comden and Adolph Green
Director: Jerome Robbins
Choreographers: Jerome Robbins and Bob Fosse
Opened: 11/29/56, New York; a run of 924 performances

Ever since appearing together in a nightclub revue, Betty Comden and Adolph Green had wanted to write a musical for their friend, Judy Holliday. The idea they eventually hit upon was to cast Miss Holliday as a meddlesome operator at a telephone answering service who gets involved with her clients' lives. She is in fact so helpful to one, a playwright in need of inspiration, that they meet, fall in love—though through it all she conceals her true identity—dance and sing in the subway, and entertain fellow New Yorkers in Central Park. At last she confesses that she's the operator, and they go off to loveland. A film version was made that is virtually the stage show on film, with Dean Martin playing opposite Miss Holliday.

The material in this section is by Stanley Green and Richard Walters, some of which was previously published elsewhere.

THE BOYS FROM SYRACUSE

Music: Richard Rodgers
Lyrics: Lorenz Hart
Book and Direction: George Abbott
Choreographer: George Balanchine
Opened: 11/23/38, New York; a run of 235 performances

The idea for *The Boys from Syracuse* began when Rodgers and Hart, while working on another show, were discussing the fact that no one had yet done a musical based on Shakespeare. Their obvious choice was *The Comedy of Errors,* chiefly because Hart's brother Teddy Hart was always being confused with another comic actor, Jimmy Savo. Set in Ephesus in ancinet Asia Minor, the ribald tale concerns the efforts of two boys from Syracuse, Antipholus and and his servant Dromio, to find their long-lost twins, also named Antipholus and Dromio. Complications arise when the wives of the Ephesians, Adriana and her servant Luce, mistake the strangers for their husbands. An Off-Broadway revival had a run of 502 performances in 1963. A movie was made of the musical in 1940.

CAN-CAN

Music and Lyrics: Cole Porter
Book and Direction: Abe Burrows
Choreographer: Michael Kidd
Opened: 5/7/53, New York; a run of 892 performances

Next to *Kiss Me, Kate, Can-Can* was Cole Porter's most successful Broadway musical. To make sure that his script would be grounded on the true origins of the scandalous dance known as the can-can, librettist Abe Burrows traveled to Paris where he studied the records of the courts, the police, and the Chamber of Deputies. In the story he came up with, set in 1893, La Mome Pistache, owner of the Bal du Paradis, is distresed about the investigation of her establishment because of the lively and scandalous dance performed there. She uses her wiles to attract the stern Judge Aristide Forestier, who has been appointed to the investigation, but eventually they fall in love, and they and the can-can live happily ever after.

CAROUSEL

Music: Richard Rodgers
Lyrics and Book: Oscar Hammerstein II
Director: Rouben Mamoulian
Choreographer: Agnes de Mille
Opened: 4/19/45, New York; a run of 890 performances

The collaborators of *Oklahoma!* chose Ferenc Molnar's Liliom as the basis for their second show and best score. Oscar Hammerstein shifted Molnar's Budapest locale to a late 19th century fishing village in New England. The two principal roles are Billy Bigelow, a carnival barker, and Julie Jordan, an ordinary factory worker. Besides Billy's famous "Soliloquy," his other solo is "The Highest Judge of All," which he sings after his death on earth before facing his maker. Even though the tessitura is high in the role, this is definitely for a high, virile baritone, and not a tenor.

DO RE MI

Music: Jule Styne
Lyrics: Betty Comden and Adolph Green
Book and Direction: Garson Kanin
Choreographers: Marc Breaux and Deedee Wood
Opened: 12/26/60, New York; a run of 400 performances

A wild satire on the ways in which the underworld muscled in on the jukebox business, *Do Re Mi* was adapted by Kanin from his own novel. With characters reminiscent of the raffish denizens of *Guys and Dolls,* the show offered two of Broadway's top clowns of the era: Phil Silvers as a fast-talking, would-be bigshot, and Nancy Walker as his long suffering spouse.

GENTLEMEN PREFER BLONDES

Music: Jule Styne
Lyrics: Leo Robin
Book: Joseph Stein and Anita Loos
Director: John C. Wilson
Choreographer: Agnes de Mille
Opened: 12/8/49, New York; a run of 740 performances

A satirical look at the 1920s, the musical is based on Anita Loos' novel and play of the same name. Carol Channing, in her first starring role on Broadway, played the gold-digging girl from Little Rock, who in action mostly on board an ocean liner headed to France, meets a number of accomodating gentlemen. A new stage version of the musical, called *Lorelei,* opened in 1974, with 10 songs from the original score plus new ones by Styne, Comden and Green. With Carol Channing again as the star the revision ran 320 performances. A screen version of the musical, with Jane Russel and Marilyn Monroe, was released in 1953.

GUYS AND DOLLS

Music and Lyrics: Frank Loesser
Book: Abe Burrows and Jo Swerling
Director: George S. Kaufman
Choreographer: Michael Kidd
Opened: 11/24/50, New York; a run of 1,200 performances

Populated by the hard-shelled but soft-centered characters who inhabit the world of writer Damon Runyon, this "Musical Fable of Broadway" tells the tale of how Miss Sarah Brown of the Save-a-Soul Mission saves the souls of assorted Times Square riff-raff while losing her heart to the smooth-talking gambler, Sky Masterson. A more comic romance involves Nathan Detroit, who runs the "oldest established permanent floating crap game in New York," and Miss Adelaide, the star of the Hot Box nightclub, to whom he has been engaged for fourteen years. The gambler Sky sings "My Time of Day" in the dark hours just before dawn to Sarah, his unlikely girlfriend from the Salvation Army. In "Luck Be a Lady Tonight" Sky has bet on a roll of the dice that if he wins, the losers will pay him not in money, but with their souls—they'll have to show up at the mission prayer meeting, which keeps the mission open and Sarah happy and in the neighborhood. "More I Cannot Wish You" is sung as a song of blessing by Arvide, Sarah's paternal fellow mission worker, to her about following her heart and loving Sky.

Guys and Dolls played on Broadway for 239 performances with an all black cast in 1976. In 1992, an enormously successful revival opened in New York, and a new cast recording was made of the show. The 1955 film version stars Frank Sinatra, Marlon Brando, Jean Simmons, and Vivian Blaine (the original Miss Adelaide).

JESUS CHRIST SUPERSTAR

Music: Andrew Lloyd Webber
Lyrics: Tim Rice
Director: Tom O'Horgan
Opened: 10/12/71, New York; a run of 711 performances

Though conceived as a theatre piece, the young team of Lloyd Webber and Rice could not find a producer interested in the "rock opera." Instead, they recorded it as an album, which became a smash hit. Concert tours of the show, which is an eclectic telling of the final week in the life of Jesus, followed, and it didn't take any more convincing that this would fly in the theatre. Despite some mixed press about the production and some objections from religious groups, the piece had its appeal, particularly among the young. The show broke all records in London. The concept of a "rock opera" caused quite a stir at the time, and had its effect on the through-sung shows to follow, such as *Evita, Cats, Song and Dance, Les Misérables* and *The Phantom of the Opera.*

KISMET

Music and Lyrics: Robert Wright and George Forrest based on Alexander Borodin
Book: Charles Lederer and Luther Davis
Director: Albert Marre
Choreographer: Jack Cole
Opened: 12/3/53, New York; a run of 583 performances

The story of *Kismet* was adapted from Edward Knoblock's play first presented in New York in 1911 as a vehicle for Otis Skinner. The music of *Kismet* was adapted from themes by Alexander Borodin, from such works as the "Polovitsian Dances" and "In the Steppes of Central Asia." The musical's action occurs within a twenty-four hour period from dawn to dawn, in and around ancient Baghdad, where a Public Poet (first played by Alfred Drake), assumes the identity of Jauu the beggar and gets into all sorts of Arabian Nights adventures. At the end of the day, he is elevated to the position of Emir of Baghdad. His daughter, Marsinah, sings "And This Is My Beloved" to the young Prince Caliph, her new husband. The film version was made by MGM in 1955. A new recording of the musical was released in 1992 with opera star Samuel Ramey in the role of the poet.

KISS ME, KATE

Music and Lyrics: Cole Porter
Book: Samuel and Bella Spewack
Director: John C. Wilson
Choreographer: Hanya Holm
Opened: 12/30/48, New York; a run of 1,077 performances

The genesis of Cole Porter's longest-running musical occurred in 1935 when producer Saint Subber, then a stagehand for the Theatre Guild's production of Shakespeare's *The Taming of the Shrew,* became aware that its stars Alfred Lunt and Lynn Fontanne, quarreled almost as much in private as did the characters in the play. Years later he offered this parallel story as the basis for a musical comedy to the same writing trio, Porter and the Spewacks, who had already worked on the successful show, *Leave It to Me!* The entire action of *Kiss Me, Kate* occurs backstage and onstage at Ford's Theatre, Baltimore, during a tryout of a musical version of *The Taming of the Shrew.* The main plot concerns the egotistical actor-producer Fred Graham and his temperamental ex-wife Lili Vanessi who —like Shakespeare's Petruchio and Kate— fight and make up and eventually demonstrate their enduring affection for each other. One of the chief features of the score is the skillful way Cole Porter combined his own musical world (songs like "So in Love," "Too Darn Hot," "Why Can't You Behave?") with a Shakespearean world (songs like "I Hate Men"). A screen version from MGM was released in 1953.

KNICKERBOCKER HOLIDAY

Music: Kurt Weill
Lyrics and Book: Maxwell Anderson
Director: Joshua Logan
Opened: 10/19/38, New York; a run of 168 performances

In spite of its relatively short run, *Knickerbocker Holdiay* is considered a significant milestone on Broadway. In one of the first musicals to use a historical subject to comment on contemporary political problems, its anti-facist theme pitted democracy against totalitarianism in retelling the reign of Governor Stuyvesant in New Amsterdam in 1647. The story tells how the governor intervenes on behalf of an independent and troublesome knife sharpener, Brom Broeck who has been arbitrarily selected by the council to the executed on a trumped up charge, mainly because they had no one to hang. The musical is one of the first of Kurt Weill's American shows.

LITTLE MARY SUNSHINE

Music, Lyrics and Book: Rick Besoyan
Directors: Ray Harrison and Rick Besoyan
Choreographer: Ray Harrison
Opened: 11/18/59, New York (Off Broadway); a run of 1,143 performances

Little Mary Sunshine, a witty, melodious takeoff of the *Naughty Marietta/Rose-Marie/*Jeannette MacDonald-Nelson Eddy school of operetta, was initially presented at a nightclub some three years before the long-running production opened Off Broadway. The story is set in the Colorado Rockies early in the century, and deals with the romance between the mincing heroine and stalwart Captain Big Jim Warrington, who saves his beloved from the clutches of a treacherous Indian just in time for their "Colorado Love Call" duet.

A LITTLE NIGHT MUSIC

Music and Lyrics: Stephen Sondheim
Book: Hugh Wheeler
Director: Harold Prince
Choreographer: Patricia Birch
Opened: 2/25/73, New York; a run of 601 performances

Based on Ingmar Bergman's 1955 film, *Smiles of a Summer Night,* the score for *A Little Night Music* is composed in 3 (3/4, 3/8, 9/8, etc.), and contains Sondheim's biggest hit song, "Send in the Clowns." The show is a sophisticated, somewhat jaded look at a group of well-to-do Swedes at the turn of the century, among them a lawyer, Fredrik Egerman, his virginal child-bride, Anne, his former mistress, the actress Desirée Armfeldt, Desirée's current lover, the aristocratic Count Carl-Magnus Malcolm, the count's suicidal wife, other guests and some witty servants. Eventually, the proper partners are sorted out during a weekend party at the country house of Desirée's mother, a former concubine of European nobility. A film version, with a change of locale to Vienna, was released in 1978.

MACK AND MABEL

Music and Lyrics: Jerry Herman
Book: Michael Stewart
Director and Choreographer: Gower Champion
Opened: 10/6/74, New York; a run of 65 performances

Set in the silent film era, this musical is based on the romance of Mack Sennett and Mabel Normand, whom Sennett transformed from Brooklyn waitress to movie star. "I Won't Send Roses" is Mack's unsentimental-sentimental song to Mabel at the beginning of their relationship. The show starred Robert Preston and Bernadette Peters on Broadway.

ME AND MY GIRL

Music: Noel Gay
Lyrics: Various
Book: L. Arthur Rose and Douglas Furber, revised by Stephen Fry
Opened: 1937, London; a run of 1,646 performances
       new production 8/10/86, New York

The Cockney character of Bill Snibson originated in 1935 in *Twenty to One,* played by comedian Lupino Lane. The actor became so attached to the part that he initiated a new musical show built around Bill two years later, resulting in *Me and My Girl*, a light social class comedy. Revivals came to London in 1941, 1945 and 1949. A charming, old-fashioned song and dance show, the principal part was played both in London, where the new production opened in 1985, and New York by Robert Lindsay to great acclaim.

MERRILY WE ROLL ALONG

Music and Lyrics: Stephen Sondheim
Book: George Furth
Director: Harold Prince
Choreographer: Larry Fuller
Opened: 11/16/81, New York; a run of 16 performances

Founded on the George S. Kaufman-Moss Hart play of the same name, *Merrily We Roll Along* is an innovative conception in that it tells its tale backwards—from the present when Franklin Shepard is a rich, famous, but morally compromised film producer and composer, to his idealistic youth when he graduated from high school. The story centers around the enduring and changing friendship between 3 people. The Broadway production was not a success, but the tuneful score has gained a following. The songwriter characters' hit song in the show's plot is "Good Thing Going."

LES MISÉRABLES

Music: Claude-Michel Schönberg
Lyrics: Herbert Kretzmer and Alain Boublil
Original French Text: Alain Boublil and Jean-Marc Natel
Directors: Trevor Nunn and John Caird
Choreographer: Kate Flatt
Opened: 9/80, Paris; an initial run of 3 months
10/8/85, London; still running as of 6/1/93
3/12/87, New York; still running as of 6/1/93

Les Misérables lends a pop opera texture to the 1200 page Victor Hugo epic novel of social injustice and the plight of the downtrodden. The original Parisian version contained only a few songs, and many more were added when the show opened in London. Thus, most of the show's songs were originally written in English. The plot is too rich to capsulize, but centers on Jean Valjean, who has go to prison in previous years for stealing a loaf of bread, and takes place over several years in the first half of the 19th century. "Empty Chairs at Empty Tables" is sung by Marius after most of his companions are killed in the student uprisings of 1832 in Paris. "Stars" is Javert's song of determined pursuit of Valjean.

MLLE. MODISTE

Music: Victor Herbert
Lyrics and Book: Henry Blossom
Director: Fred Latham
Opened: 12/25/05, New York; a run of 202 performances

The operetta inaugurated the partnership of composer Victor Herbert and Henry Blossom, resulting in seven more shows together. Set in Paris, the show is about a stagestruck girl, Fifi, who works in a hat shop. A wealthy American comes along and helps Fifi become a famous singer, and of course, they fall in love. The show was revived on Broadway 5 times, the last in 1929.

THE MOST HAPPY FELLA

Music, Lyrics and Book: Frank Loesser
Director: Joseph Anthony
Choreographer: Dania Krupska
Opened: 5/3/56, New York; a run of 676 performances

Adapted from Sidney Howard's Pulitzer Prize-winning play, *They Knew What They Wanted,* Loesser's musical was a particularly ambitious work for the Broadway theatre, with more than thirty separate musical numbers, including arias, duets, trios, quartets, choral pieces, and recitatives. Robust, emotional expressions (such as "Joey, Joey, Joey" and "My Heart Is So Full of You") were interspersed with more traditional specialty numbers (such as "Big D" and "Standing on the Corner"), though in the manner of an opera, the program credits did not list individual selections. In the story, set in California's Napa Valley, an aging vinyard owner (originally played by opera singer Robert Weede) proposes by mail to a waitress he calls Rosabella. She accepts, but is so upset to find Tony old and fat, and on their wedding night she allows herself to be seduced by Joe, the handsome ranch foreman. Once he discovers that his wife is to have another man's child, Tony threatens to kill Joe, but there is a reconciliaton and the vintner offers to raise the child as his own. A 1979 Broadway revival, starring Giorgio Tozzi, ran for 52 performances. A more successful revival ran in New York in 1991-2, resulting in a new recording of the score.

MY FAIR LADY

Music: Frederick Loewe
Lyrics and Book: Alan Jay Lerner
Director: Moss Hart
Choreographer: Hanya Holm
Opened: 3/15/56, New York; a run of 2,717 performances

The most celebrated musical of the 1950s began as an idea of Hungarian film producer Gabriel Pascal, who devoted the last two years of his life trying to find writers to adapt George Bernard Shaw's play, *Pygmalion,* into a stage musical. The team of Lerner and Loewe also saw the possibilities, particularly when they realized that they could use most of the original dialogue and simply expand the action to include scenes at the Ascot Races and the Embassy Ball. They were also scupulous in maintaining the Shavian flavor in their songs, most apparent in such pieces as "Get Me to the Church on Time," "Just You Wait," Why Can't the English?," "Show Me," and "Without You." Shaw's concern with class distinction and his belief that barriers would fall if all Englishmen would learn to speak properly was conveyed through a story about Eliza Doolittle (a star making role for Julie Andrews), a scruffy flower seller in London's Covent Garden, taken on as a speech student of linguistics Professor Henry Higgins (played by Rex Harrison) to increase her social and economic potential. Eliza succeeds so well that she outgrows her social station and —in a development added by librettist Lerner— even makes Higgins fall in love with her. Though the record was subsequently broken, *My Fair Lady* became the longest running production in Broadway history, remaining for over six and a half years. The show was also a solid success in London. For the 1964 movie version, Julie Andrews was passed over for Audrey Hepburn as Eliza (whose singing was dubbed by Marni Nixon), along with Harrison. Two major revivals have been mounted in New York as of this writing. In 1976 the musical ran for 377 performances with Ian Richardson and Christine Andreas. In 1981 New York again saw Rex Harrison in 119 performances with Nancy Ringham's Eliza. In the late 1980s a new recording of the musical was released with Kiri Te Kanawa and Jeremy Irons in the leading roles.

NINE

Music and Lyrics: Maury Yeston
Book: Arthur Kopit, Mario Fratti
Director: Tommy Tune
Choreographers: Tommy Tune and Thommie Walsh
Opened: 5/9/92, New York; a run of 732 performances

The influence of the director-choreographer was emphasized again with Tommy Tune's highly stylized, visually striking production of *Nine,* which, besides being a feast for the eyes is also one of the very few non-Sondheim Broadway scores to have true musical substance and merit from the 1970s and 1980s. The musical evolved from Yeston's fascination with Federico Fellini's semi-autobiographical 1963 film *8 1/2.* The story spotlights Guido Contini (Raul Julia), a celebrated but tormented director in a mid-life crisis who has come to a Venetian spa for a rest, and his relationships with his wife, his mistress, his protégé, his producer, and his mother. The production, which flashes back to Guido's youth and also takes place in his imagination, offered such inventive touches as an overture in which Guido conducts his women as if they were instruments, and an impressiontic version of the Folies Bergères. "Guido's Song" is at the top of the show. "Only With You" shows Guido's indecision about the women in his life.

OKLAHOMA!

Music: Richard Rodgers
Lyrics and Book: Oscar Hammerstein II
Director: Rouben Mamoulian
Choreographer: Agnes de Mille
Opened: 3/31/43, New York; a run of 2,212 performances

Oklahoma! is the most important, recognized landmark in the development of musical theatre in America. Rodgers could not interest his longtime partner, Lorenz Hart, in the project, and he reluctantly began writing his first show with Hammerstein. A fusion of song, story, character, and dance created an example of a "book" show that was unified and dramatically sophisticated compared to most of the song and dance entertainments of the 1920s and 1930s. Based on the Lynn Riggs play, *Green Grow the Lilacs,* the story is set among the ranchers on the prairie near the turn of the century. Curly wants to take Laurey to the box social, but she hasn't given him an answer. The menacing Jud would like to take Laurey himself, and in a moment of confusion and revenge, she chooses Jud over Curly. But things sort out, Laurey and Curley are married, and Jud is accidentally killed. Oklahoma becomes a state, and a happy ending for all (except poor Jud). The show was modern in concept, and also set a modern standard for length of a run, setting a record that would hold up for 15 years. It toured for over 10 years, a returned to Broadway twice during the 1950s. A revival ran 293 shows in New York in 1979. The movie version was released in 1955.

OLIVER!

Music, Lyrics and Book: Lionel Bart
Director: Peter Coe
Opened: 6/30/60, London; a run of 2,618 performances
  1/6/63, New York; a run of 744 performances

Oliver! established Lionel Bart as Britain's outstanding musical theatre talent of the 1960s when the musical opened in London. Until overtaken by *Jesus Christ Superstar, Oliver!* set the record as the longest running musical in British history. Based on Charles Dickens' novel about the orphan Oliver Twist and his adventures as one of Fagin's pickpocketing crew, *Oliver!* also had the longest run of any British musical present in New York in the 1960s. The show was revived on Broadway in 1984. In 1968, it was made into an Academy Award winning movie produced by Columbia. "My Name" is the menacing Bill Sykes entrance song.

ON THE TOWN

Music: Leonard Bernstein
Lyrics and Book: Betty Comden and Adolph Green
Director: George Abbott
Choreographer: Jerome Robbins
Opened: 12/28/44, New York; a run of 463 performances

Based on the Bernstein-Robbins ballet *Fancy Free, On the Town* marked the Broadway debut of four major talents: composer Leonard Bernstein, writers Betty Comden and Adolph Green, and choreographer Jerome Robbins. Three sailors with a one day pass explore New York become involved with three girls, whirling through the day at the Museum of Natural History, Central Park, Times Square, a nightclub, and on Coney Island. Besides "Lonely Town," the show's most familiar tune is "New York, New York." The musical has been revived on in 1959 Off-Broadway, and in 1971 on Broadway. The movie version was released in 1949, starring Gene Kelly, Frank Sinatra, Vera-Ellen, and Betty Garrett. A new, complete recording of the show has also been made in recent years.

PIPE DREAM

Music: Richard Rodgers
Lyrics and Book: Oscar Hammerstein II
Director: Harold Clurman
Choreographer: Boris Runanin
Opened: 11/30/55, New York; a run of 246 performances

Adapted from John Steinbeck's novel *Sweet Thursday,* the sixth Rodgers and Hammerstein show presented the skid row inhabitants of Cannery Row in Monterey, California. A disappointment, both critically and commercially, the show represented a lukewarm string of 3 shows in the 1950s by the creators compared their previous midas touch with *Oklahoma!, Carousel, South Pacific* and *The King and I.* The plot is mostly about Doc, a marine biologist, whose romance with a pretty vagabond named Suzy is abetted by Fauna, the warmhearted madam of a local bordello.

PROMISES, PROMISES

Music: Burt Bacharach
Lyrics: Hal David
Book: Neil Simon
Director: Robert Moore
Choreographer: Michael Bennett
Opened: 12/1/68, New York; a run of 1,281 performances

Two of the most successful songwriters of the 1960s, Bacharach and David teamed up with the equally successful Neil Simon to create a unique show, adapted from the 1960 movie, *The Apartment*. Like other shows of the era, the setting was the business world, and the inability of the bachelor leading character to say no to his superiors when they want to use his apartment for their extramarital recreation.

SHE LOVES ME

Music: Jerry Bock
Lyrics: Sheldon Harnick
Book: Joe Masteroff
Director: Harold Prince
Choreographer: Carol Haney
Opened: 4/23/63, New York; a run of 301 performances

The closely integrated, melody drenched score of *She Loves Me* is certainly one of the best ever written for a musical comedy. It was based on a Hungarian play, *Parfumerie,* by Miklos Laszlo, that had already been used as the basis for two films, *The Shop Around the Corner* and *In the Good Old Summertime* (changed to an American setting). Set in the 1930s in what could only be Budapest, the tale is of the people who work in Maraczek's Parfumerie, principally the constantly quabbling sales clerk Amalia Balash (Barbara Cook) and the manager Georg Nowack (Daniel Massey). It is soon revealed that they are anonymous pen pals who agree to meet one night at the Café Imperiale, though neither knows the other's identity. One of the more extroverted and sportier male employees at the parfumerie is smitten with a fellow female clerk, thus "Ilona." The show is well represented on the original cast album, which on two disks preserves practically every note of the show's music.

SILK STOCKINGS

Music and Lyrics: Cole Porter
Book: George S. Kaufman, Leueen McGrath and Abe Burrows
Director: Cy Feuer
Choreographer: Eugene Loring
Opened: 2/24/55, New York; a run of 478 performances

Cole Porter's last Broadway musical was based on the popular MGM film, *Ninotchka*, in which Greta Garbo was seen as a stern-faced Russian official who succumbs to the charms of both Paris and a French count. In the musical, Ninotchka is again seduced by the city and a man, though this time he is an American talent agent involved in getting a Russian composer to write the score for a movie version of *War and Peace*. A movie version of the musical was released in 1957 starring Fred Astaire.

Music: Kurt Weill
Lyrics: Langston Hughes
Book: Elmer Rice
Director: Charles Friedman
Opened: 1/9/47, New York; a run of 148 performances

Kurt Weill persuaded Elmer Rice to write the libretto based on his own Pulitzer Prize winning play, with poet Langston Hughes supplying the powerful and imaginative lyrics. Billed as a "dramatic musical," the blending of the score's drama and music is very close to opera. In fact, the show has found it's most suitable home in the opera house. The story is a collection of characters who live in a tenement walk-up in a blue collar neighborhood of Manhattan. Rose Maurrant is a young adult woman still living at home, and she works in an office with the extroverted Harry Easter. Though married, Harry likes to have his fun, and in "Wouldn't You Like to Be on Broadway" tries to seduce Rose.

THE UNSINKABLE MOLLY BROWN

Music and Lyrics: Meredith Willson
Book: Richard Morris
Director: Dore Schary
Choreographer: Peter Gennaro
Opened: 11/3/60, New York; a run of 532 performances

The Unsinkable Molly Brown retold the saga of a near-legendary figure of the Colorado silver mines who pulled herself up from poverty by her unswerving determination and by marry a lucky prospector, "Leadville" Johnny Brown. While still penniless, Johnny declares to Molly that he'll "Never Say No." They strike it rich, and he doesn't, giving her every gauche thing her heart desires. A screen version was released in 1964.

WHERE'S CHARLEY

Music and Lyrics: Frank Loesser
Book and Direction: George Abbott
Choreographer: George Balanchine
Opened: 10/11/48, New York; a run of 792 performances

The show was based on Brandon Thomas' 1892 London hit, *Charley's Aunt*, one of the most durable farces in the English language. The first Broadway production to have a score by Frank Loesser, the show was a star vehicle for top dancing clown, Ray Bolger. At Oxford, Charley and his friend wish to entertain their lady friends, but need a chaperon, supplied by Charley playing his own aunt in a pinch. Then darn it if the real woman doesn't show up. The movie version also starred Bolger and was released in 1952. Amy is the object of Charley's affection, by the way.

THE GIRL THAT I MARRY

from *Annie Get Your Gun*

Words and Music by
IRVING BERLIN

Tempo di Valse

The girl that I mar-ry will have to be as soft and as pink as a nurs-er-y. The girl I call my own ____ will wear sat-ins and lac-es and smell of col-ogne. Her nails will be pol-ished and in her

MY DEFENSES ARE DOWN

from *Annie Get Your Gun*

Music & Lyrics by
IRVING BERLIN

fen - ses are down, __ I might as well sur-ren - der, for the bat - tle can't be

won. But I must con - fess that I like it, so there's

noth - ing to be done, Yes, I must con - fess that I

like it, be - ing mis - 'ra-ble is gon - na be fun!

ALL THROUGH THE NIGHT

from *Anything Goes*

Words and Music by
COLE PORTER

me,

You're nev - er there at all, _____

I know _____ you've for - sak - en

me

Till the shad - ows fall; _____

But then _____ once a - gain _____

LONG BEFORE I KNEW YOU
from *Bells are Ringing*

Lyrics by BETTY COMDEN
and ADOLPH GREEN
Music by JULE STYNE

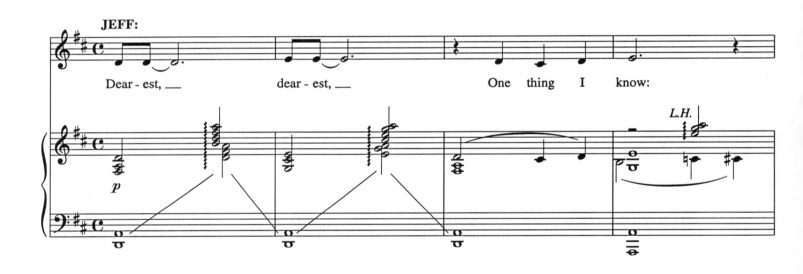

JEFF:
Dear - est, ____ dear - est, ____ One thing I know:

Ev - 'ry-thing I feel for you start - ed man - y a - ges a - go. ____

long be-fore I held you, ____ Long be-fore I kissed you, ____

Long be-fore I touched you ____ and felt this glow. ____ But now you

real - ly are here and now at last I know That long be-fore I knew you, ____

I loved you so.

JUST IN TIME
from *Bells Are Ringing*

Words by BETTY COMDEN
and ADOLPH GREEN
Music by JULE STYNE

I was some-thing dragged in by the cat. then

Moderato

Just in time, _____

_____ I found you just in time. _____ Be - fore you

came, my time _____ was run-ning low.

I was lost, The los - ing dice were tossed. My brid - ges

all were crossed, No where to go.

Now you're here And now I know just where I'm go - ing; No more

To Coda ⊕
2nd time slowly

doubt or fear, I've found my way. For love came

D.S. al Coda

CODA

IT'S ALL RIGHT WITH ME
from *Can-Can*

Words and Music by
COLE PORTER

you want to for-get some-one too?_____ It's the wrong game_____ with the wrong chips,_____ Though your lips are tempt-ing, they're the wrong lips,___ They're not her lips, but they're such tempt-ing lips,___ That if some night___ you're free,_____ Dear, it's all right,___ It's all right___ with me._____

ff

THIS CAN'T BE LOVE
from *The Boys from Syracuse*

Words by LORENZ HART
Music by RICHARD RODGERS

love and then he died of it,

In 4

Poor half - wit!

mp
rall.

Moderately - In 2

This can't be love be - cause I feel so well, ___ No

sobs, no sor - rows, no sighs. ___

p

THE HIGHEST JUDGE OF ALL

from *Carousel*

Lyrics by OSCAR HAMMERSTEIN II
Music by RICHARD RODGERS

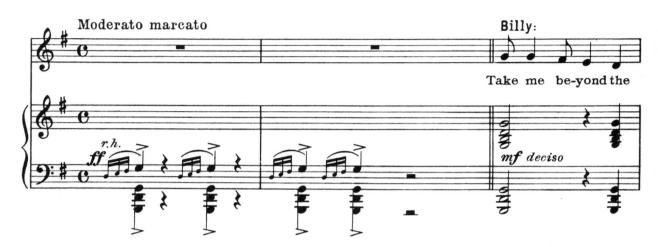

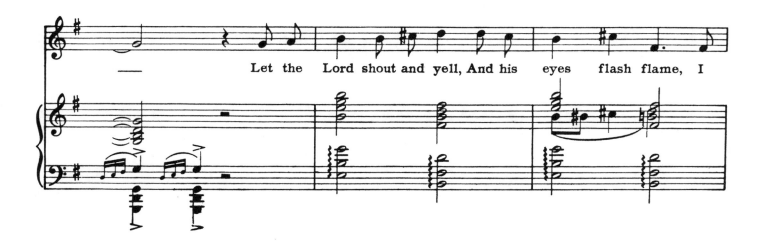

Let the Lord shout and yell, And his eyes flash flame, I

prom-ise not to quiv-er when he calls my name. Let him send me to hell, But be-

fore I go, I feel that I'm en-ti-tled to a hell of a show!

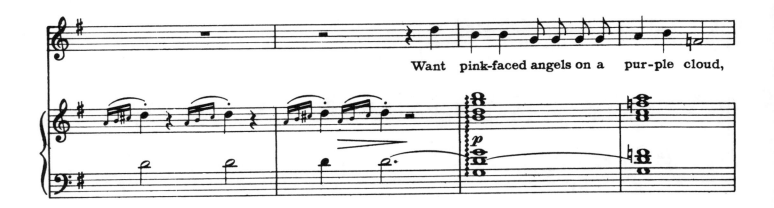

Want pink-faced angels on a pur-ple cloud,

Twang-in' on their harps till their fin-gers get red. Want or - gan mu-sic, let it

roll out loud, Roll - in' like a wave, wash-in' ov - er my head! Want

ALL OF MY LIFE
from *Do Re Mi*

Words by BETTY COMDEN
and ADOLPH GREEN
Music by JULE STYNE

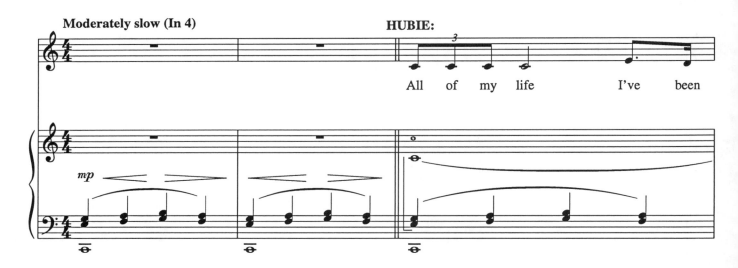

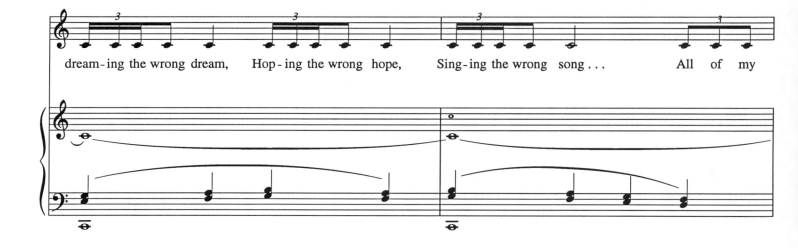

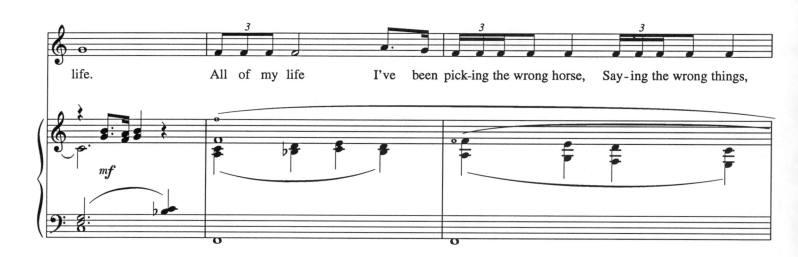

Mak-ing the wrong bets . . . All of my life.

L'istesso tempo (In 2)

I thought there was

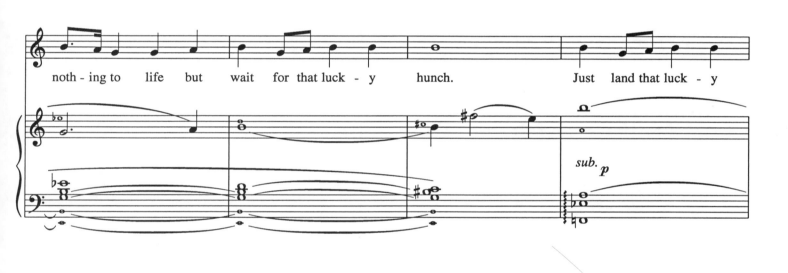

noth - ing to life but wait for that luck - y hunch. Just land that luck - y

sub. p

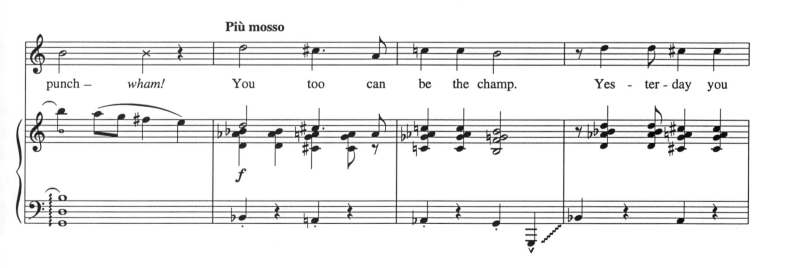

Più mosso

punch — *wham!* You too can be the champ. Yes - ter - day you

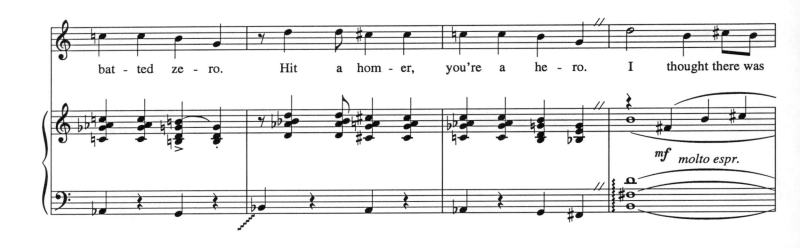

bat - ted ze - ro. Hit a hom - er, you're a he - ro. I thought there was

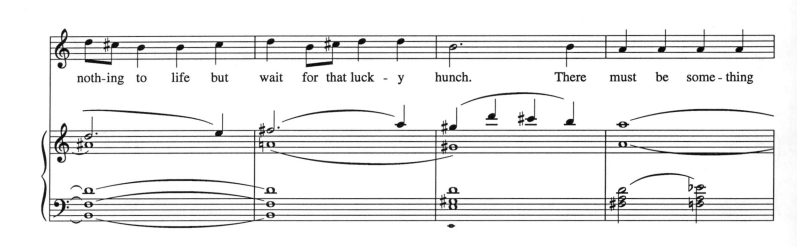

noth-ing to life but wait for that luck - y hunch. There must be some-thing

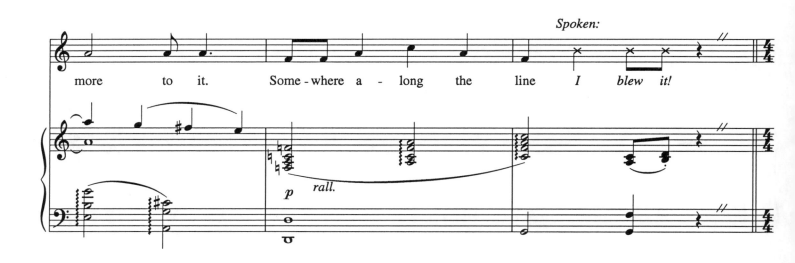

more to it. Some-where a - long the line *I blew it!*

Tempo I (In 4)

All of my life   I've been see-ing the wrong crowd,   wear-ing the wrong ties,

Danc-ing the wrong steps,   All of my life.   All of my life   I've been

off on the wrong beam, Back-ing the wrong team, Dream-ing the wrong dream,   All of my life   All of my

Very slow

life,   All   of my no good life._____

mf *poco rall.*   *ppp*   *mf*

I   thought the A - mer - i-can dream was: Wait for your one big   break.

Più mosso

Just give the dice a shake.   You   too   can be on top.

sub.   *p*   *f tutti*

Be an o-ver night sen-sa-tion, Meet the press and face the na-tion.

Poco meno mosso

I thought the A-mer-i-can dream was: Wait for your one big

break. There must be some-thing more to it,

Some-where a-long the line *I blew it.* All of my life I've been

Spoken:　　　　　　　　　　**Tempo I (In 4)**

learn-ing the wrong tricks,   Pull-ing the wrong strings,   Mak-ing the wrong moves,   All   of   my

life.   All of my life   I've been off on the wrong beam,   Back-ing the wrong team,

Dream-ing the wrong dream.   All of my life,   All of my   life,

Broader

All   of my whole damn   life. _____

BYE BYE BABY
from *Gentlemen Prefer Blondes*

Words and Music by
LEO ROBIN and JULE STYNE

When they give you the eye. _____ Al-though I
know that you care, __ Won't you write __ and de-clare __ That
though on the loose, __ You are still __ on the square. __
I'll be gloom-y, But send that rain-bow to me

Then my shad-ows will fly,_____ Though you'll be

gone for a-while__ I know that I'll be smil-ing With my

ba-by bye and bye.   bye,_____ With my

ba-by_____ bye and bye._____

MY TIME OF DAY
from *Guys and Dolls*

Words and Music by
FRANK LOESSER

LUCK BE A LADY

from *Guys and Dolls*

Words and Music by
FRANK LOESSER

SKY: *(freely and dramatically)*

They call you "La - dy Luck" But there is room for doubt. At times you have a ve - ry un - la - dy - like way of run - ning out You're on this date with me. The pick - ings have been

Luck let a gen - tle - man see _____

How nice a dame you can be _____

I know the way you've treat - ed oth - er guys ___ you've been with,

Luck be a la - dy with me! _____

dice. _____ So let's keep the par - ty po - lite. _

____ Nev - er get out of my sight _

____ Stick with me ba - by I'm the

fel - low you came in with. Luck be a la - dy,

Luck be a la - dy.

Luck be a la - dy to - night. ___

Luck, let a gen - tle - man see. ___

How nice a dame you can be. ___

MORE I CANNOT WISH YOU

from *Guys and Dolls*

By FRANK LOESSER

call-ing cards_ up - on a sil - ver tray _____ But more I can-not wish__ you than to

wish you find your love, ___ Your own true love, this day _____

Stand - ing there _____ Gaz-ing at you _____ Full ___ of the

bloom ___ of youth Stand- ing there _____ Gaz-ing at you___

__ With the sheep's eye _____ And the lick-er-ish tooth

Mu-sic I can wish you, mer-ry mu-sic while you're young,___ And wis-dom, when your

hair has turned to gray_____ But more I can-not wish___ you than to

wish you find your love,___ Your own true love,___ this day___

With the sheep's eye And the lick-er-ish tooth And the

strong arms to car-ry you a - way._____

PILATE'S DREAM
from *Jesus Christ Superstar*

Lyrics by TIM RICE
Music by ANDREW LLOYD WEBBER

Moderately slow

Bbm   Ebm   Ab7
I dreamed I met a Gal-i-le-an A

Bbm   Cb   F7   F7+
most a-maz-ing man __ He had that look __ you

Gb   Ebm6   F7
ver-y rare-ly find   The haunt-ing hunt-ed

FATE
from *Kismet*

Words and Music by
ROBERT WRIGHT
and GEORGE FORREST
(music based on themes of A. BORODIN)

THE POET:

Fate! Fate can be the trap in your path, The bit-ter cup of your tears, Your wine of wrath!

Fate can be shade in the des - ert blaze, Sud-den food in a fam - ine

(Freely)

found, The sound of praise! In-com-pre-hen-si-ble and

Tempo I

strange, Fate can play a trick with the twine To weave the e - vil and

sempre marcato il basso

good In one de - sign! And

poco a poco accel.

so, my Des-ti - ny, I look at you and can-not see Is it

cresc.

f

Fate

sfz > mp
R.H.

__ can play a trick with the twine __

To weave the e - vil and good __ In

one _____ de - sign! _____

_____ And so, _____ my Des - ti -

ny, _____ I look at you _____ and can - not

see Is it good, is it ill? Am I

blessed, am I cursed? Is it hon - ey on my

tongue or brine?

What fate, what fate

sfz

mf

is mine?

I'VE COME TO WIVE IT WEALTHILY IN PADUA

from *Kiss Me, Kate*

Words and Music by
COLE PORTER

come to wive it wealth - i - ly in Pa - du - a. _____

I heard you say "Gad - zooks, com-plete - ly mad you are." _____ 'Twould-n't

give me the slight - est shock, If her knees, now and then, should knock, If her

eyes were a wee bit crossed, Were she wear - ing the hair she'd lost, Still the

dam - sel I'll make my dame, In the dark they are all the same. I've

come to wive it wealth - i - ly in Pa - du - a.

fight like a rag-ing boar? I have oft stuck a pig be-fore. I've

come to wive it wealth-i-ly in Pa-du-a. With a

Hun-ny, nun-ny, nun-ny, And a hey, hey, hey, Not to men-tion mon-ey, mon-ey, For a

rain-y day. I've come to wive it wealth-i-ly in Pa-du-a.

THERE'S NOWHERE TO GO BUT UP

from *Knickerbocker Holiday*

Words by MAXWELL ANDERSON
Music by KURT WEILL

ly, _____ No as-sets, no cap-i-tal, noth-ing but
ly, _____ For pret-ty near-ly ev-'ry-thing's hap-pened to

me. When your shoes need sol-ing, and you're stand-ing
me!

on the town, _____ And your girl says please for-

get her, When you're on rock bot-tom, and you

p

L.H.

has - been, Then there's no - where to go but up! To the man who has a - plen - ty an - y change is for the worse, So he plays a los - ing hand a - gainst the u - ni - verse, ___ But in win - try weath - er, when the

p

Can't go this way, Then there's

no - where to go but up!

2. TENPIN:

Up one up!

YOU'RE THE FAIREST FLOWER

from *Little Mary Sunshine*

Music and Lyrics by
RICK BESOYAN

In this bow - er, dear, _____ You're the frail - est blos -

-som, Gos - sa - mer. _____ 'Though you're such a

shy Miss, Shy Miss, I dis - close; _____ You're the

fair - est flow - er on earth, An A - mer - i - can Beau - ty Rose. _____

IN PRAISE OF WOMEN
from *A Little Night Music*

Music and Lyrics by
STEPHEN SONDHEIM

(C.M.:) The pa-pers... He men-tioned pa-pers, Some le-gal pa-pers which I did-n't see there... Where were they? The god-damn pa-pers she had to sign? What non-sense... He brought her pa-pers, They were im-por-tant so he had to be there. I'll

I WON'T SEND ROSES
from *Mack and Mabel*

Music and Lyric by
JERRY HERMAN

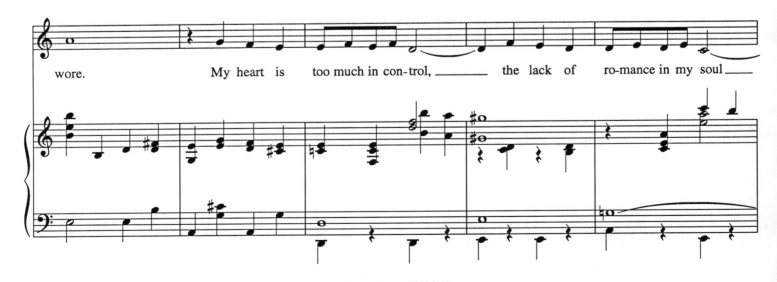

Will turn you gray, kid, so stay a - way, kid. For - get my

shoul - der when you're in need. For - get - ting birth-days

is guar - an - teed._____ And should I love you, you would be the last to

know._____ I won't send ros - es And ros - es suit

LEANING ON A LAMP-POST

from *Me and My Girl*

Words and Music by
NOEL GAY

ab - so - lute - ly won - der - ful and mar - vel - ous and beau - ti - ful, __ And an - y - one __ can un - der - stand

why I'm lean - ing on a lamp - post at the cor - ner of the street, In case a

cer - tain lit - tle la - dy comes by. _____

Grazioso

* opt. just play top note

GOOD THING GOING

from *Merrily We Roll Along*

Music and Lyrics by
STEPHEN SONDHEIM

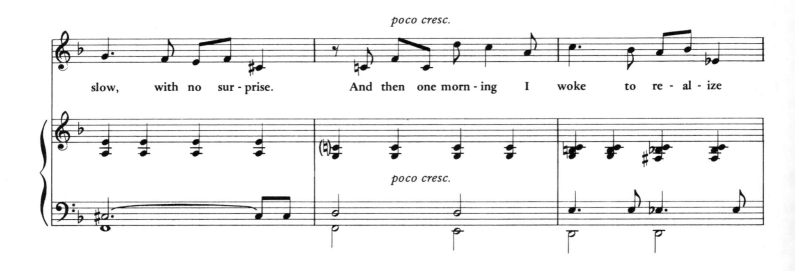

We had a good thing go - ing.

It's not that noth - ing went wrong. Some an - gry mo - ments, of course, but just a few, And on - ly mo - ments, no more, be - cause we knew We had this good thing go - ing.

Strict tempo, non più mosso

And if I want-ed too much, _____ Was that such _____ A mis-take _____

_____ At the time? _____

You nev-er want-ed e-nough, _____ All right, tough, _____ I don't make _____

_____ That a crime. _____

poco rit.   a tempo

In - stead of just kept on.___

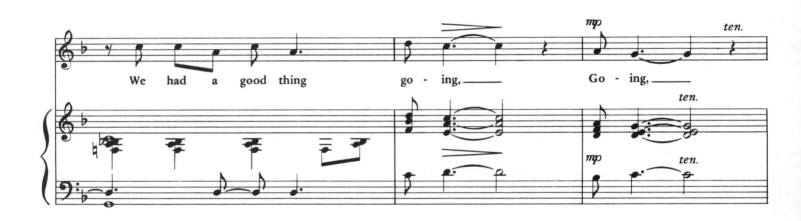

We had a good thing go - ing,___ Go - ing,___

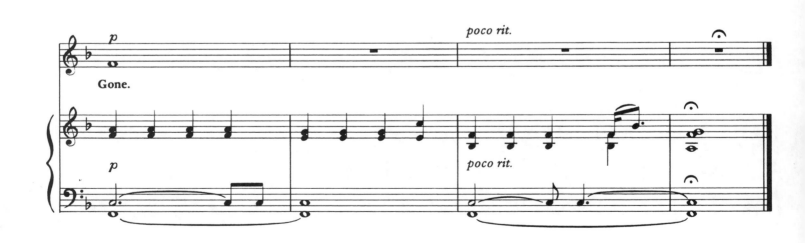

Gone.

JOEY, JOEY, JOEY

from *The Most Happy Fella*

By FRANK LOESSER

Or may-be A - ri - zo - na sug-ar beet.___ The

wind blows in _____ and she sings to me, 'Cause

I'm one of her ram-blin' kin.___ She sings:

A tempo

Jo - ey,___ Jo - ey, Jo - ey.___

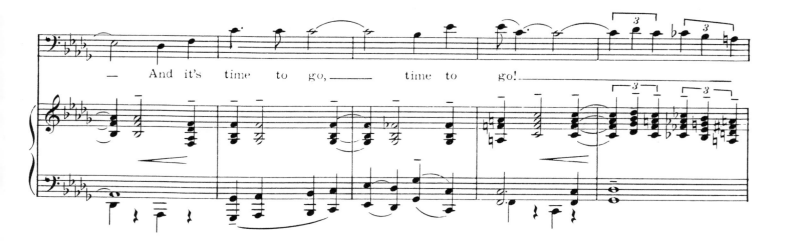

And it's time to go,_____ time to go!

Jo - ey,_____ Jo - ey, Joe!_____

EMPTY CHAIRS AT EMPTY TABLES

(The Café Song)

from *Les Misérables*

Lyrics by HERBERT KRETZMER
and ALAIN BOUBLIL
Music by CLAUDE-MICHEL SCHÖNBERG

Here it was they lit the flame.____ Here they sang a-bout to - mor-row, and to -

mor - row nev - er came.

Più mosso

From the ta - ble in the

cor - ner they could see a world re - born__ And they rose with voi - ces

ring-ing. And I can hear them now. The ver - y words that they had

STARS
from *Les Misérables*

Lyrics by HERBERT KRETZMER
and ALAIN BOUBLIL
Music by CLAUDE-MICHEL SCHÖNBERG

aim. And each in your sea-son re-turns and re-turns and is al-ways the

same. And if you fall as Lu-ci-fer fell, you

cresc. *mf*

rall. *a tempo*

fall _____ in flame! And so it has been, and so it is writ-ten on the

f *f* *mp* *f*

door - ways to par-a-dise, _____ that those who fal-ter and those who fall _____ must

132

GUIDO'S SONG

from *Nine*

Lyrics and Music by
MAURY YESTON

prob - lem __ es - pe - cial - ly when my bod - y's clear - ing

for - ty as my mind is near - ing ten. I can hard - ly stay

up, and I can't get to sleep, and I don't want to

wake to - mor - row morn - ing at the bot - tom of some heap, but why

take it so se - ri - ous - ly? Af - ter

all there's noth-ing at stake here— on - ly me! I want to be

young, and I want to be old. I would like to be

wise be - fore my time, and yet, be fool - ish and brash and bold— I would like the

u - ni - verse   to get down on its knees and say "Gui - do,   what - ev - er you please, it's o -

kay e - ven if it's im - pos - si - ble, we'll ar - range   it..."

cresc.   *f*   *mp*

That's all that I   want.

rit.

rit.

I am lust - ing for

here (with a coun-ter-)here (mel-o-dy in the) here (top___ of the morn-ing to you,

Gui-do) Gui-do (Gui-do) Gui-do (Gui-do) Gui-do.

(Me) Me (Me) I want to be Proust! or the Mar-quis de

Sade. I would like to be Christ, Mo-ham-med, Bud-dha, but not

id - i - ot went and told, I would like the u - ni - verse to get down on its knees and say

"Gui - do, what-ev - er you please, it's o - kay e - ven if it's ri - dic - u - lous, we'll ar -

molto rit.   *a tempo*

range it. . ."   SO AR - RANGE   IT! _____

That's all that I want.

ONLY WITH YOU

from *Nine*

Lyrics and Music by
MAURY YESTON

Each verse of the song is sung to a different woman

I WANT WHAT I WANT
WHEN I WANT IT

from *Mlle. Modiste*

Lyrics by HENRY BLOSSOM
Music by VICTOR HERBERT

wife. _____ I drink my fill, if I have the will, with
all. _____ Of course, your life, if you have no wife, is

poco meno.

friends who are tried and old, ____ And oft, when the com-pa-ny's
lone-some at times and slow, ____ But wheth-er you mar-ry or

marcato.

a tempo.

good, I stay; I may not come home till the break of day, But if
not, they say, You're bound to re-gret ____ it ei-ther way; Let

accel.   *rit*   *molto marcato.*

din-ner is wait-ing and I am a-way, There is no one to nag me or
those who are sin-gle be sor-ry who may, I'd be sor-ri-er mar-ried I

p accel.   *rit*   *p molto cresc.*

I'VE GROWN ACCUSTOMED TO HER FACE

from *My Fair Lady*

Words by ALAN JAY LERNER
Music by FREDERICK LOEWE

153

rene - ly in - de - pend - ent and con - tent be - fore we met; (Fl., Hp.)

Sure - ly I could al - ways be that way a - gain and yet I've grown ac -
(Vln. A) (Solo Vln.)
pp

cus - tomed to her looks; Ac - cus - tomed to her voice: Ac -
p (Str., W.W., Hp.)

cus - tomed to her face.
f (W.W., Hns., Trpts.) *rit*

HIGGINS: Marry Freddy! What an infantile idea! What a heartless, wicked, brainless thing to do. But
she'll regret it. It's doomed before they even take the vow!

158

THE SURREY WITH THE FRINGE ON TOP

from *Oklahoma!*

Lyrics by OSCAR HAMMERSTEIN II
Music by RICHARD RODGERS

Nos - ey - pokes -'ll peek thru their shut-ters and their eyes will pop! The wheels are yel-ler, the up-hol-ster-y's brown, The dash-board's gen-u-ine leath-er, With i-sin-glass cur-tains y' can roll right down, in case there's a change in the weath - er.

Two bright side lights, wink - in' and blink - in' Ain't no fin - er rig, I'm a - think - in'! You c'n keep yer rig if you're think - in' 'at I'd keer to swop fer that shin - y lit - tle sur - rey with the fringe on the top!

Brightly

I would say the fringe was made of silk _____

Would-n't have no oth-er kind but silk _____

It has real-ly got a team of snow-white hors - es

One's like snow, the oth-er's more like milk. _____

Stgs.
W. W.

poco rit.

+ Hns. Guit.
mod.^{to} marcato

The lyrics at these two spots have been altered just slightly for a solo singer version. The top line of the page, sung by Aunt Eller in the show, is "Would you say the fringe was made of silk?" The third line, sung by Laurey in the show, is "Has it really got a team of snow-white horses?"

Con sentimento (*slowly*)

I can see the stars git-tin' blur-ry When we ride back home in the sur-rey, Rid - in' slow - ly home in the sur-rey with the fringe on top. I can feel the day git-tin' old-er, Feel a sleep-y-head near my shoul-der,

Nod-din', droop-in' close to my shoul-der till it falls, ker-

plop! The sun is swim-min' on the rim of a hill, The

moon is tak-in' a head-er, And jist as I'm think-in' all the

earth is still, A lark-'ll wake up in the med-der.

ALL AT ONCE YOU LOVE HER

from *Pipe Dream*

Lyrics by OSCAR HAMMERSTEIN II
Music by RICHARD RODGERS

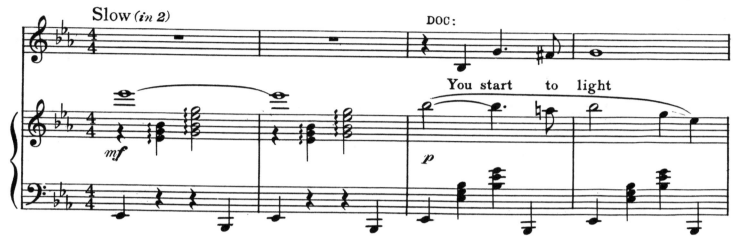

But all at once You love her. You like her

eyes, You tell her so. She thinks you're

wise And clev - er. You kiss good-

night   And then you know   You'll kiss good-night   For-

ev - er!   You won - der where   your heart can

go   And all at once you know.

THE MAN I USED TO BE
from *Pipe Dream*

Lyrics by OSCAR HAMMERSTEIN II
Music by RICHARD RODGERS

Schottische tempo

The man I used to be, A hap-py man was he, And aim-less as a leaf in a gale. _ What-ev-er has be-come of that light-heart-ed bum _ Who thought he had the world by the tail? _ The man I used to be, His life was gay and free And aim-less as a cloud in the sky. _

MY NAME
from the Columbia Pictures-Romulus film *Oliver!*

Words and Music by
LIONEL BART

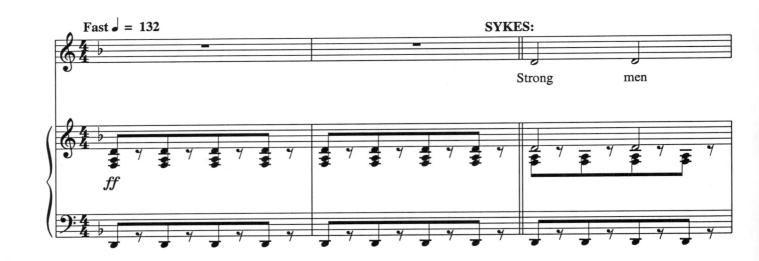

Strong men trem - ble when they hear it!

They've got cause e-nough to fear it! It's much

black - er than they smear it! No - bod - y men - tions... My name!

Some toff slum - ming wiv' his val - et, Bump'd in -

LONELY TOWN

from *On the Town*

Words by BETTY COMDEN
and ADOLPH GREEN
Music by LEONARD BERNSTEIN

Ga-bey's com-in', Ga-bey's com-in' to town,__ So what? Who cares? Back on the ship it seemed such a snap: You'd tap a girl on the shoul-der,

world's an emp-ty place, _____ And ev-'ry town's _____ a lone-ly town. _____

Un-less there's love,

ILONA
from *She Loves Me*

Lyrics by SHELDON HARNICK
Music by JERRY BOCK

How I en- vy you each eve- 'ning, when work is through, For

Rubato

I have on- ly me to be with while you have you. With-

A Tempo

out you, _____ Il- o- na, _____ How

cold my lone- ly life has grown. _____ Are you

ie. _____ Mis - tle - toe, I long for some - one,

please tell me who. Like some di - vine di - vin - ing rod, it

*(kiss) **Rubato**   **A Tempo**

points straight to you. Re - mem - ber, _____ Il -

o - na. _____ The sun - ny nights we knew be -

* Kodaly kisses the air, or blows a kiss.

gen - er - ate a spark that's rare. _____ Why de-

ny that it's there, Il - o - - na, _____ You

feel it, _____ I know. _____ Let's help it _____

to glow. _____

ALL OF YOU
from *Silk Stockings*

Words and Music by
COLE PORTER

Fox trot tempo

(with bounce, but not too fast)

After watch-ing her ap-peal from ev-'ry an-gle,

There's a big ro-man-tic deal I've got to wan-gle.

For I've fal-len for a

WOULDN'T YOU LIKE TO BE ON BROADWAY

from *Street Scene*

Lyrics by LANGSTON HUGHES
Music by KURT WEILL

Allegro non troppo *(ben ritmato)*

HARRY EASTER: *with an insinuating, tempting rhythm*

Would-n't you like to be on Broad-way And go danc-ing at the Zan-zi-bar? And have your-self an up-and-com-ing boy friend Who can make an-y course in par? Hey, kid?

*Throughout ♩♪ is literally played ♩ ♪ (swing beat).

glow? Would-n't you like to be the lead-ing la - dy In my

heart, But al - so in some Broad-way show __ Would-n't you like some per-son-al pro-

mo - tion To a niche on the Great White Way?

Would-n't you? Hey kid? *How a-bout it?* *Hey kid?* Would-n't you like to be on Broad-

Would-n't you like to have two maids

Scrub-bing your shoul - der blades in a bub-ble bath's sweet per-fume?

Can't you hear the door-man at the stage door: "Here's your car!"

When we leave your dress-ing room?

Would-n't you like to have the crowds ap-plaud you

At your

I'LL NEVER SAY NO
from *The Unsinkable Molly Brown*

Words and Music by
MEREDITH WILLSON

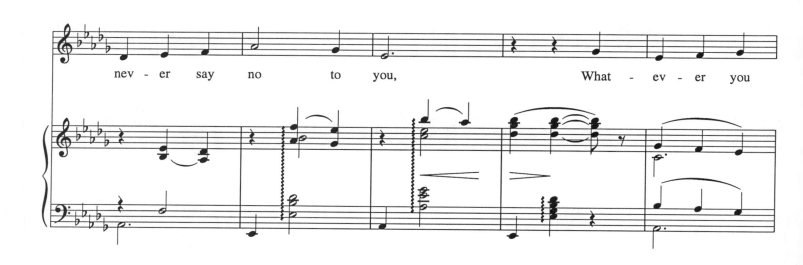

You know I'll glad-ly wait for a life-time or two... Just to look at you.

Tempo, but freely

I'll smile when you say: "Be glad." I'll

weep if you want me sad. ___ To-day is to-mor-row, if

you want it so. I'll stay or I'll go, ___

ONCE IN LOVE WITH AMY

from *Where's Charley?*

By FRANK LOESSER

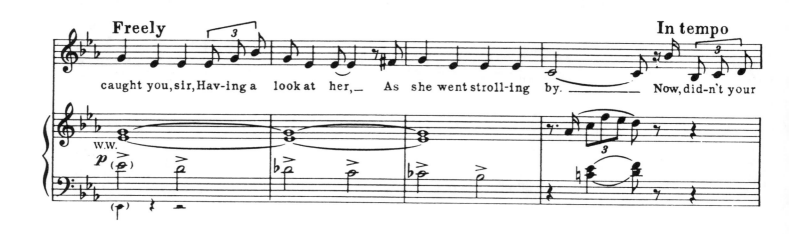

PROMISES, PROMISES

from *Promises, Promises*

Lyrics by HAL DAVID
Music by BURT BACHARACH

my kind of prom - is - es _____ Can lead to

joy and hope and love, _____ Yes,

love! _____